DISNEY · PIXAR

TOY STORY

THE RETURN OF BUZZ LIGHTYEAR

WRITER:
JESSE BLAZE SNIDER

ART:
NATHAN WATSON
(CHAPTER 1-4)

INKS:
NATHAN WATSON,
MIKE DECARLO,
JUAN CASTRO
(CHAPTER 4)

LETTERER:
MARSHALL DILLON
(CHAPTER 1)

DERON BENNETT
(CHAPTERS 2-4)

COLOURS:
MICKEY CLAUSEN
(CHAPTER 1-4)
ERIC COBAIN
(CHAPTER 4)

COVER:
MICHAEL CAVALLARO
DESIGNER:
ERIKA TERRIQUEZ

EDITOR:
AARON SPARROW

SPECIAL EDITION COVERS 2A & 2B:
NATHAN WATSON
COLOURS: VERONICA GANDINI

Published by Panini Publishing, a division of Panini UK. Office of publication: Panini UK, Brockbourne House, 77 Mount Ephraim, Tunbridge Wells, Kent TN4 8BS. No part of this book may be reproduced or tra~~ electronic or mechanical, including pho~~ d retrieval system, without written permis~~

DISNEY
POCKET STORIES

PANINI

AB   D1424805

1952740

CHAPTER 1

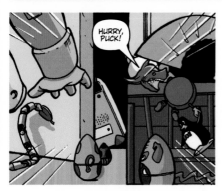

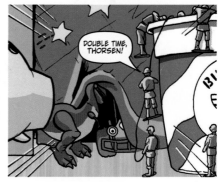

I WONDER WHAT SHE GOT ME?!

MAYBE XR OR *BOOSTER!*

OR MAYBE EVEN EMPEROR ZURG! OR...

THERE GOES THE NEIGHBORHOOD...

WELL THEN, YOU'RE LUCKY YOUR GRANDMOTHER GAVE ME A GIFT RECEIPT!

...

AW, MOM... I ALREADY HAVE THIS ONE.

NOW, IF YOU GO CALL HER RIGHT NOW AND THANK HER FOR THE WONDERFUL PRESENT SHE GOT YOU, WHICH YOU ABSOLUTELY DID *NOT* HAVE, I'LL TAKE YOU TO TOY MANIA TONIGHT AND WE CAN RETURN IT AND GET SOMETHING NEW.

I'LL CALL HER RIGHT NOW. THANKS MOM. YOU'RE THE BEST!!!

ANDY, HOW MANY TIMES HAVE I TOLD YOU NOT TO RUN DOWN THE STAIRS?!

SORRY, MOM.

WHAT'S A *"GIFT RECEIPT"*? AND WHAT DOES SHE MEAN *"RETURN IT AND GET SOMETHING NEW?"* YOU CAN DO THAT?!

YEAH, BUZZ...YOU CAN.

THAT JUST SEEMS... *WRONG*.

IT'S LIKE THE POOR TOY NEVER EVEN HAD A CHANCE...

TRUST ME BUZZ...IT'S FOR THE BEST.

"FOR THE BEST?" I THOUGHT YOU'D BE ON MY SIDE.

I *AM* ON YOUR SIDE.

OBVIOUSLY *NOT*, WOODY.

I'M GOING TO MEET OUR GUEST BEFORE IT'S TOO LATE. HE CAME IN A *"STAR COMMAND"* BOX, IT'S ONLY RIGHT THAT I BE THE TOY TO BREAK THE BAD NEWS.

THAT'S *NOT* A GOOD IDEA BUZZ, YOU'VE GOTTA TRUST ME ON THIS!

WHOEVER'S UP THERE IS ABOUT TO GET *"RETURNED"* AND I DON'T KNOW ABOUT YOU, BUT THAT SOUNDS LIKE THE MOST TERRIFYING THING THAT COULD HAPPEN TO A TOY!

YOU KNOW, YOU'RE ABSOLUTELY RIGHT BUZZ, AND AS ONE OF THE OLDEST TOYS IN ANDY'S ROOM, I THINK THAT *I* SHOULD HANDLE IT...*ALONE*.

WELL... EXCEPT MAYBE SID...

COME ON WOODY. STILL SCARED I'M GOING TO STEAL YOUR THUNDER?

OF COURSE NOT, IT'S JUST... WELL, YOU DON'T KNOW WHAT'S UP THERE!

YOU'RE RIGHT. THAT'S WHY I'M GOING UP THERE TO FIND OUT!

OH...

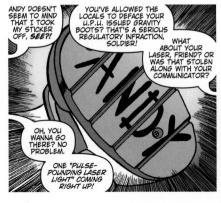

KRAK
KRAK
KRAK

AAGH! MY EYES!

POKE!

HEY, LET'S KEEP IT CLEAN! THERE ARE *PRE-SCHOOL* TOYS IN THE ROOM!

KLK

~CHOKE~!!

WAY TO GO, BUZZ!

THAT'S THE OLDEST TRICK IN THE BOOK... AND YOU *FELL* FOR IT!

~CHOKE~!!

~WEEZ~!!

~GACK~!!

HEY... THE AIR IS FINE! YOU CAN BREATHE! I'M BREATHING... *SEE?*

I CAN BREATHE... *SEE!*

NEW GUY?

IS HE ALL RIGHT?

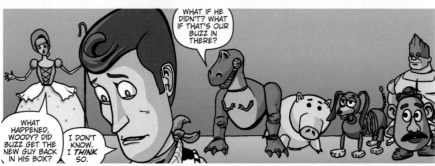

WHAT IF HE DIDN'T? WHAT IF THAT'S OUR BUZZ IN THERE?

WHAT HAPPENED, WOODY? DID BUZZ GET THE NEW GUY BACK IN HIS BOX?

I DON'T KNOW. I *THINK* SO.

I DON'T KNOW.

WHAT ARE WE GONNA DO?

WE'LL JUST HAVE TO WAIT AND SEE.

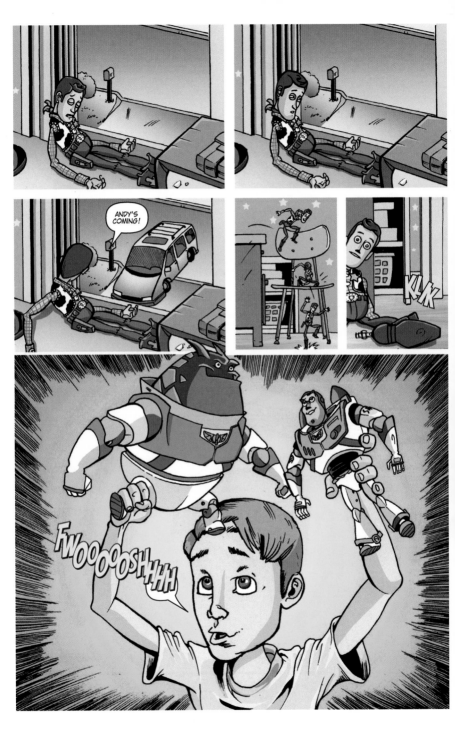

CHAPTER 2

PSST... COMMANDER LIGHTYEAR! COME HERE!

IS THAT YOU, WOODY?

YEAH, IT'S ME. I'VE CALLED AN EMERGENCY PLAYROOM MEETING, SO HURRY UP!

COME ON BOOSTER, WE DON'T WANT TO BE LATE.

RIGHT AWAY, SIR! SORRY!

HELLO? WHERE ARE YOU GUYS?!

WE'RE UNDER THE BED!

IN THE DARK? HOW CAN YOU SEE?

WE HAVE... SPECIAL...NIGHT VISION GOGGLES! DON'T YOU?

OF...COURSE WE DO! NIGHT VISION GOGGLES ARE STANDARD EQUIPMENT FOR *ALL* STAR COMMAND PERSONNEL.

I DIDN'T GET NIGHT VISION GOGGLES.

ER...? OF COURSE NOT. I MEANT THAT THEY'RE STANDARD EQUIPMENT FOR ALL *ELITE* STAR COMMAND PERSONNEL.

CAN I HOLD YOUR HAND? I'M AFRAID OF THE DARK.

THAT'S WHY YOU'RE NOT A MEMBER OF THE ELITE.

AT EASE, EVERYONE. I'D LIKE TO INTRODUCE YOU TO OUR NEW RECRUIT BOO--

AAH!

THUD

CRASH

SMACK

UM, YOU SEE, *YOUR COMMANDER* WAS SENT HERE AS AN...*AMBASSADOR* FROM STAR COMMAND, BUT WE ALREADY *HAD* AN AMBASSADOR FROM STAR COMMAND. OUR AMBASSADOR WAS TRANSFERRED BACK BY MISTAKE...*SO NOW...WE* HAVE TO TAKE YOUR COMMANDER BACK TO THE *SPACE STATION,* SO WE CAN GET OUR AMBASSADOR BACK!

UNDERSTAND?

COMPLETELY.

THOSE MIND WORMS *REALLY* GOT AHOLD OF YOU.

GAH!!! YOU KNOW WHAT?! YOU'RE RIGHT! I *HAVE* BEEN POSSESSED BY A ZAMBONIAN MIND WORM! IN FACT, WE *ALL* WERE! AND IF YOU DON'T TAKE US BACK TO THE TOY STORE RIGHT NOW...

SPACE STATION.

...TAKE US BACK TO THE SPACE STATION *RIGHT NOW...* REX IS GOING TO *EAT* YOU!

BUT WOODY...I'M A *VEGETARIAN!*

≡SIGH≡ I KNOW *YOU* ARE, BUT YOUR MIND WORM...*ISN'T!*

OHHH... RIIIGHT.

MMMMM... I...*LOVE... MEAT!!!*

DELICIOUS... EXOTIC...NEW KINDS OF... ALIEN...UH, MEAT?!

I'LL DO ANYTHING YOU WANT! JUST KEEP HIM AWAY FROM ME!

GOOD BOY. ALL RIGHT, TOYS AND GIRLS--LET'S *DO THIS!*

SO, WHAT'S THE PLAN WOODY?

SARGE AND HIS MEN ARE ALREADY DOWNSTAIRS GETTING THE KEYS TO ANDY'S MOM'S CAR. REX...HAMM... SLINKY...POTATO...AND BOOSTER, YOU'RE WITH ME.

BO, YOU'RE IN CHARGE OF THE PLAYROOM UNTIL WE GET BACK.

YOU GOT IT, WOODY.

WHEEZY, IF ANYTHING GOES WRONG, YOU'RE OUR DIVERSION.

UH-OH... I KNOW WHAT *THAT* MEANS...

ROCKY, PICK UP "COMMANDER LIGHTYEAR" HERE...AND WELCOME TO THE "A" TEAM!

WHAT?!

HOLD ON HERE, WOODY! ROCKY?! I HEARD A RUMOR THAT A COMBAT CARL ONCE GOT 'IM IN A KUNG-FU GRIP AND *ROCKY* RIPPED HIS ARM CLEAN OFF!

IT'S *NOT A RUMOR.*

SEE?!

WELL THEN, SLINK... I'D SUGGEST YOU DON'T USE ANY OF YOUR ACTION FEATURES AGAINST HIM.

THAT'S NOT FUNNY, WOODY! THIS IS SERIOUS!!!

LOOK, YOU'RE RIGHT, SLINK. ROCKY CAN BE A BIT... *UNPREDICTABLE.* BUT THE FACT IS THAT WITHOUT BUZZ, WE'RE DOWN A MAN, AND HIS SPECIAL... HOW SHALL I SAY... *TALENTS* MIGHT COME IN HANDY.

ARFF?!

BUSTER! WHEEZY, YOU KNOW WHAT *THAT* MEANS...

YEAH...I *DO.*

ARFF!

WELL, YOU CAN THANK *ROCKY* FOR YOUR NIGHT AS A CHEW TOY.

MAKE SURE YOU CLOSE THE DOOR ONCE YOU GET HIM IN THE ROOM!

WHO'S A GOOD BOY? YOU WANNA PLAY? YOU WANNA PLAY...

...FETCH?

≶SQUEAK-SQUEAK!≶

YOU LIKE THE SQUEAKY TOY?!

THEN GO GET IT!

THE THINGS I DO FOR YOU GUYS...

≶SQUEAK-SQUEAK!≶

SLAM!

HOPEFULLY YOU DIDN'T WAKE THE WHOLE *NEIGHBORHOOD!* YOU'RE LUCKY ANDY'S MOM IS A SOUND SLEEPER!

NOW, GET DOWNSTAIRS... *QUIETLY.*

MOMENTS LATER...

ALL RIGHT, THE *FRONT DOOR* WAS ONE THING, BUT THE *CAR* DOOR WAS GOIN' TOO FAR!

GIRLY TOY.

YOU BET I AM, ROCKY! IF I GET A *KINK* IN MY SLINK, IT AIN'T EVER COMIN' OUT!!!

DO *YOU* KNOW HOW TO *FIX* A *BROKEN* SLINKY?

NO! OF COURSE NOT! NO ONE DOES! A SLINKY *BREAKS...* AND THEY JUST THROW IT OUT AND BUY A NEW ONE! WELL, THAT AIN'T HAPPENIN' TO *ME!* NO-SIR-REE-BOB, WE'RE JUST GONNA HAVE TO FIGURE OUT ANOTHER WAY TO OPEN DOORS FROM NOW ON!

GIRLY TOY.

YOU KNOW, I LIKED YOU BETTER WHEN YOU DIDN'T TALK.

MIKE? WHAT ARE YOU DOIN' OUT HERE IN THE CAR?

ANDY LEFT ME HERE AFTER HIS FRIEND'S KARAOKE PARTY. WHY IS BUZZ ALL TIED UP? WHAT'S GOING ON?

THAT'S NOT BUZZ! Y'SEE, BUZZ KNOCKED BUZZ OUT AND GOT BUZZ RETURNED TO THE TOY STORE, SO WE'RE TAKING BUZZ BACK SO WE CAN RESCUE BUZZ!

FORGET I ASKED.

HEY WOODY, NOT THAT *THIS* ISN'T ENTERTAINING, BUT ARE YOU PLANNING ON, I DON'T KNOW, *DRIVING* US SOMEWHERE ANYTIME SOON?

YEAH, WE'RE BURNING MOONLIGHT HERE!

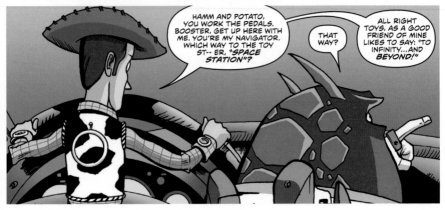

...HOW *SLOW* YOU WERE GOING?

WHAT?!

ALL RIGHT, GET IT TOGETHER ROOKIE. THERE'S A PERFECTLY GOOD EXPLANATION FOR THIS.

WHAA?! ALL RIGHT... *FREEZE!*

CHA-CHUNK!

WHO'S THERE?

...WHERE IN THE HECK?

RUSTLE   RUSTLE

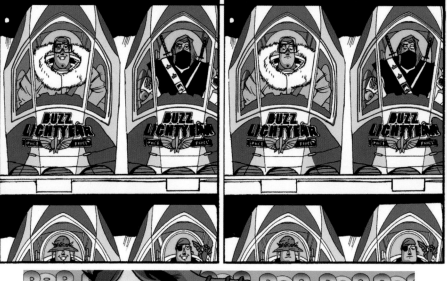

CHAPTER 3

TOYMANIA TOY STORE. NIGHT.

WHO DID I THINK I WAS KIDDING, ANYWAY?

WHAT WOULD ANDY WANT WITH A TOY THAT DOESN'T EVEN *WORK* ANYMORE?

KA-CHIP

I GUESS I'D HAVE RETURNED ME *TOO*.

"*TO INFINITY AND BEYOND!!!*"

APPARENTLY I'M NOT THE *ONLY* ONE WHO'S MALFUNCTIONING...

SOMEBODY HEL--*UNGH!*

SLAM!

MOUNT PLUSHMORE

THAT DOESN'T EVEN MAKE ANY SENSE! WHY WOULD THERE BE *CAVEMEN...* IN *SPACE?!*

LEAVE ME ALONE YOU *CAVE...* SPACEMEN!

HEY!

WHAT'S THE BIG IDEA, PAL?

SHFF!

OH NO! YOU FOUND ME!

I DIDN'T FIND *YOU!* I FOUND *A HIDING SPOT!!!*

BUT THIS IS *MY* HIDING SPOT!

YOU DON'T *NEED* A HIDING SPOT. THESE TOYS ARE ON *YOUR* SIDE!

BUT I DON'T *KNOW* THAT! THIS WHOLE EXPERIENCE IS GIVING ME *SERIOUS* TRUST ISSUES!

GET OUTTA HERE, BEFORE ONE OF THOSE SHARP TEETH O' YOURS TEARS OUR STITCHING!

I DON'T CARE! THERE'S A WHOLE CLAN OF CAVE-SPACEMEN OUT THERE AND I'M *STAYING HERE* UNTIL THEY DISCOVER FIRE OR SOMETHING!

HEY GUYS! HE'S OVER *HERE!*

YOU... *SQUEALERS!* YOU'RE ALL STUFFED WITH *EVIL!*

UGG?

OOG?

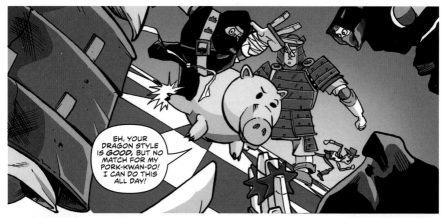

HEY, THANKS FOR COMING DOWN HERE TONIGHT. WHAT A GREAT LOOKING CROWD.

SO WE'VE GOT "ARCTIC BUZZ" HERE TONIGHT. I SEE YOU GUYS CAME PREPARED FOR A *COLD* RECEPTION. RIGHT?

OH, NEVER MIND. IT MAY BE COLD IN SPACE, BUT UNDER YOUR HELMET IT'S *ABSOLUTE ZERO!*

WHAT A HOCKEY PUCK!

LOOK EVERYONE-- IT'S "NINJA BUZZ".

WHY AREN'T YOU AN EMPTY PACKAGE? NOW *THAT* WOULD BE NINJA!

THAT'S ABOUT ALL THERE IS TO SAY ABOUT *THIS* NUMB-CHUCK!

HEY, WHO LET *SLEEPY TIME BUZZ* OUT OF HIS PACKAGE?

TO NAPTIME *AND BEYOND!*

EASY, BUDDY. SOMEBODY HIT THE SNOOZE BUTTON!

YOU KNOW, I SAW THE COMMERCIAL THAT FEATURED YOU. NOW THAT WAS ENOUGH TO PUT *ANYONE* TO SLEEP!

JUST KIDDING. NICE *SLIPPERS.*

AND WHO ARE YOU LOVELY LADIES SUPPOSED TO BE?

I'LL HAVE YOU KNOW THAT WE'RE "DISGUISE BUZZ!"

DISGUISED AS WHAT, TWISTED SISTER?!

OH, FOR CRYING OUT LOUD, YOU SPACE TOYS HAVE NO SENSE OF HUMOR!

PASSING BY THE PLAIN OLD BUZZ LIGHTYEAR...

...FOR "BATH TIME BUZZ" OR "ARCTIC BUZZ" OR "JUNGLE ATTACK BUZZ."

FINALLY, WHEN I'D LOST ALL HOPE, A PRETTY YOUNG WOMAN PICKED ME UP, SMILED AT ME AND BOUGHT ME FOR HER NEPHEW'S BIRTHDAY.

I WAS SO EXCITED-- I SWORE THAT I WOULD MAKE THAT KID HAPPIER THAN ANY TOY HE EVER GOT!

BUT HE ALREADY HAD A BUZZ LIGHTYEAR...

...AND I WAS RETURNED TO THE STORE...

...FOR THE FIRST TIME...

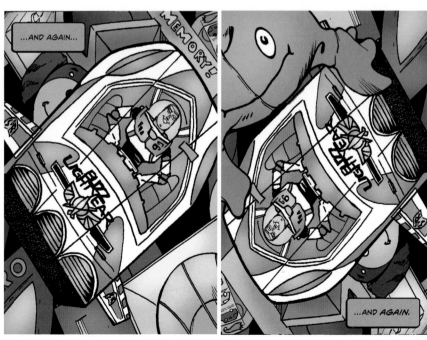

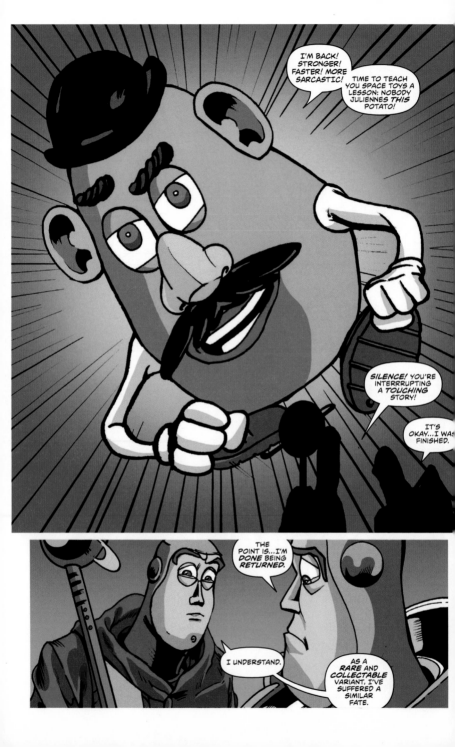

TOYS LIKE ME ARE DESTINED FOR "EBAY" AND A *LIFETIME* ON A *DISPLAY SHELF* OR *WORSE*...IN STORAGE.

WE'LL NEVER KNOW WHAT IT'S LIKE TO BE *PLAYED WITH*...

...TO BE *TRULY* LOVED.

EVERY MORNING I ARISE BEFORE OPENING TO *HIDE* FROM *COLLECTORS*, THEN SIT ON THE SHELF IN THE AFTERNOON *HOPING* TO BE SEEN AND PURCHASED BY A *CHILD*...

...BUT *WHAT* CHILD WANTS A *GLORIFIED POLITICIAN* ACTION FIGURE?

THIS RANGER JUST WANTS WHAT ANY OF US WANT. TO ENJOY OUR TIME AS A *CHILD'S BELOVED TOY.*

...AND SO I PROPOSE A CONTEST.

A *RACE* AROUND THE *WORLD!*

HE MEANS THE *STORE*, RIGHT?

I SURE *HOPE* SO.

THE WINNER GETS ANDY...AND THE GREATEST PRIZE OF ALL...

...LOVE.

DONE.

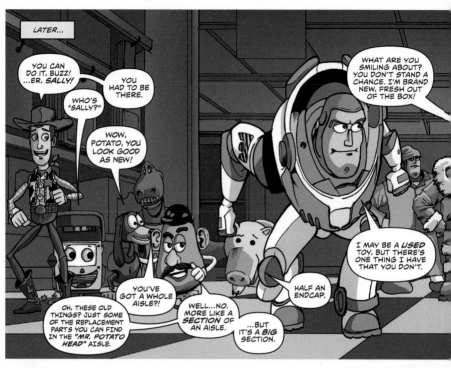

LATER...

YOU CAN DO IT, BUZZ! ...ER, SALLY!

YOU HAD TO BE THERE.

WHO'S "SALLY"?

WOW, POTATO, YOU LOOK GOOD AS NEW!

WHAT ARE YOU SMILING ABOUT? YOU DON'T STAND A CHANCE. I'M BRAND NEW, FRESH OUT OF THE BOX!

I MAY BE A USED TOY, BUT THERE'S ONE THING I HAVE THAT YOU DON'T.

YOU'VE GOT A WHOLE AISLE?!

OH, THESE OLD THINGS? JUST SOME OF THE REPLACEMENT PARTS YOU CAN FIND IN THE "MR. POTATO HEAD" AISLE.

WELL...NO. MORE LIKE A SECTION OF AN AISLE.

...BUT IT'S A BIG SECTION.

HALF AN ENDCAP.

OH? YEAH? WHAT'S THAT?

GET SET...

POP!

GO!

CHAPTER 4

I HAD THE *BEST* VIEW...AND *I* SAY *I* WON!

NO WAY! SALLY *MUST* HAVE WON. HE WAS *TACKLED* ACROSS THE *FINISH LINE!*

EH, THAT'S NOT NECESSARILY TRUE, WOODY. THOUGH HE *DID* TACKLE BUZZ, IT'S STILL POSSIBLE THAT HIS FACE, HANDS OR ARMS CROSSED THE LINE *FIRST.*

HEY, WHOSE SIDE ARE YOU ON ANYWAY?!

LISTEN, WOODY, I JUST WENT THROUGH A NEAR DEATH EXPERI-ENCE! I'M A NEW SPUD, AND I NEED TO HOLD MYSELF TO A HIGHER STANDARD OF *TRUTH* AND *JUSTICE!*

I ADMIRE YOUR HONESTY, SOLDIER!

THANKS, SARGE.

ACTUALLY, ALL THEY DID WAS REASSEMBLE YOU WITH YOUR OLD PARTS.

REALLY...?

WELL IN *THAT* CASE, THE WINNER WAS SALLY! I'D STAKE MY EYES ON IT!

YEAH, AND THOSE ARE HIS *BEST* EYES!

HOORAY FOR SALLY!

SALLY BEAT 'IM ALL RIGHT, FAIR AND SQUARE!

THE BEST TOY WON!

WILL EVERYONE *PLEASE* STOP CALLING ME *"SALLY"*?!

SORRY BUZZ... MY FAULT.

DON'T YOU HAVE SOME SORT OF *FINISH LINE CAMERA,* IN CASE OF SOMETHING LIKE *THIS?*

NOW THAT YOU MENTION IT...

...WE DO HAVE A PICTURE OF THE FINISH.

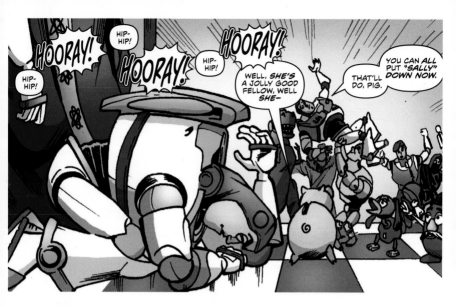

HOORAY! HIP-HIP! HIP-HIP! HOORAY! HIP-HIP! HOORAY! HIP-HIP!

WELL, *SHE'S* A JOLLY GOOD FELLOW, WELL SHE—

THAT'LL DO, PIG.

YOU CAN ALL PUT *"SALLY"* DOWN NOW.

I'M SORRY COMMANDER, BUT YOU'LL NEED TO GET BACK TO YOUR BOX IN THE *"RETURNS"* BIN.

DON'T YOU MEAN BACK TO *"CRYO-SLEEP?"*

NO SON...I'M AFRAID I *DON'T.*

AND *YOU,* SIR, ARE *FREE* TO GO. NOW, ROUND UP YOUR CREW AND GET HOME TO ANDY BEFORE HE WAKES UP.

THANK YOU SIR, WE WILL.

GOOD. AND SPACE RANGER...

YES, SIR?

RETURNS

NEVER FORGET HOW FORTUNATE YOU ARE. HE'S *NOT* THE *ONLY* TOY WHO WOULD TRADE PLACES WITH YOU IN A NANOSECOND.

...I *KNOW.*

EVERYONE ACCOUNTED FOR, SARGE?

NEGATIVE. ONE OF OUR UNIT IS AWOL, SIR!

BOOSTER'S STILL HOLED UP IN THE STUFFED TOYS. HE'S THE TOY ANDY EXCHANGED *YOU* FOR. HE'S ALSO A STAR COMMAND TOY, AND HE'S... WELL...

HAVING TROUBLE COMING TO GRIPS WITH REALITY? LET ME TALK TO HIM.

BUZZ...BE GENTLE.

ONLY *TWO* THINGS COME FROM *STAR COMMAND.* LOONIES...AND LOONIES!

YOU GOT *THAT* RIGHT.

HELLO BOOSTER, I'M—

BUZZ LIGHTYEAR OF STAR COMMAND? WHO *ISN'T?*

YEAH, WELL...I HAVE TO TELL *YOU* SOMETHING...AND I'M NOT SURE HOW YOU'RE GOING TO TAKE IT.

YOU MEAN THAT I'M A TOY?

UM...*YEAH.* WHAT GAVE IT AWAY?

I'M HIDING IN A PILE OF TEDDY BEARS IN A *TOY STORE*...I'M A COWARD, NOT AN IDIOT.

WELL, IF IT MAKES YOU FEEL ANY BETTER, YOU'RE TAKING IT *WAY* BETTER THAN I DID.

REALLY?

OH YEAH, I DRESSED UP AS A HOUSEWIFE AND THREW A TEA PARTY, BEFORE WOODY SNAPPED ME OUT OF IT...

BEING A MEMBER OF STAR COMMAND MAY HAVE TAKEN ME TO *INFINITY*...BUT IT WAS BEING ONE OF ANDY'S TOYS THAT FINALLY TOOK ME TO *INFINITY AND BEYOND.*

TAKE IT FROM A FELLOW SPACE RANGER...YOU'RE GONNA *LOVE* BEING A TOY.

MOMENTS LATER...

BOOSTER SEEMS TO HAVE TAKEN THE NEWS PRETTY WELL. WHAT'D YOU SAY TO HIM?

ALL THE SAME THINGS *YOU* SAID TO ME, WOODY.

WOW...IF ONLY "*MRS. NESBIT*" HAD TAKEN IT SO WELL...

...OR IS IT "*SALLY*" NESBIT?

WILL YOU *PLEASE*--!

I'M *KIDDING*.

IT'S GOOD TO HAVE YOU BACK, *BUZZ LIGHTYEAR.*

IT'S *GOOD TO BE BACK.*

WOODY...

...YOU THINK ANDY *WOULD* RATHER HAVE A NEW BUZZ LIGHTYEAR?

I *KNOW* HE WOULDN'T.

EH, NOT TO RUIN THIS TENDER MOMENT, WOODY, BUT HOW ARE WE SUPPOSED TO GET OUTTA HERE?

YEAH! WHEN WE CAME IN HERE, DIDN'T YOU HAVE A PLAN FOR GETTING OUT?

THAT'S A LOOOONG WAY UP, THAT'S FOR SURE!

I...HADN'T REALLY CONSIDERED THAT.

WHAT ARE WE GOING TO DO? IT'S GOING TO BE DAYLIGHT SOON! ANDY WILL WAKE UP AND MISS US!

NOW REX...AND I KNOW I SAY THIS A LOT...BUT THIS IS NO TIME TO PANIC!

WELL, IT'LL DO UNTIL ONE COMES ALONG! WHAT ARE WE GOING TO DO WHEN THE EMPLOYEES SHOW UP TO START WORK?

WAIT A MINUTE...

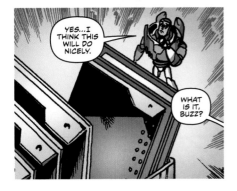

YES...I THINK THIS WILL DO NICELY.

WHAT IS IT, BUZZ?

LOOKS LIKE THEY WERE GOING TO PUT UP A NEW SHELF. IT'S HEAVY, BUT I THINK WITH OUR HELP, ROCKY SHOULD BE STRONG ENOUGH TO MOVE IT.

ALL RIGHT! BUZZ LIGHTYEAR TO THE RESCUE!

AND BUILD A LADDER! GREAT THINKING, BUZZ!

MEANWHILE...

HMM?

OH, IT'S YOU. YOU CAN SAVE YOUR LECTURE...I ALREADY KNOW WHAT I DID WAS WRONG.

THAT'S NOT WHY I'M HERE.

I CAN'T SAY I APPROVE OF WHAT YOU DID, SON...BUT I *UNDERSTAND* IT.

THERE'S NO GREATER FEELING FOR A TOY THAN TO BE LOVED BY A CHILD. IT'S WHAT WE ALL DREAM OF. WHAT WE'RE *MADE FOR.*

IT'S JUST...I FEEL LIKE I'M ONE RETURN AWAY FROM THE CLEARANCE AISLE. I WAS SO DESPERATE, I WAS WILLING TO TAKE THAT LOVE AWAY FROM ANOTHER TOY.

MAYBE I DESERVE TO BE IN THE BARGAIN BIN. I'VE DISGRACED STAR COMMAND, I'VE DISGRACED ALL OF YOU, AND I'VE DISGRACED MYSELF.

THAT'S THE GREAT THING ABOUT REMORSE, SON...

...IT MEANS IT'S *NOT TOO LATE.*

HE SACRIFICED HIMSELF TO SAVE YOU, BUZZ! OH, THE *HUMANITY!*

A MOMENT OF SILENCE, MEN...

WAIT... LOOK!

UNGHF!

5 BY 5, SPACE RANGER! NOW STOP WORRYING ABOUT ME...GET BACK TO YOUR CAR AND BE HOME WHEN ANDY WAKES UP!

GOODBYE! AND... THANKS.

UNGH...

HE'S *ALIVE!*

THANK GOODNESS!

ARE YOU ALL RIGHT DOWN THERE?

MOMENTS LATER...

WELL, THERE THEY GO. DID YOU MAKE AMENDS?

I DID...AND YOU KNOW, I FEEL A LOT BETTER!

OH!

WHAT IS IT?

I...THINK YOU SHOULD HAVE A LOOK.

WH- WHAT...?!

NO, NO, NO!

NO ONE WILL *EVER* WANT *ME* NOW.

LATER THAT MORNING...

DING-DONG!

ANDY, CAN YOU GET THE DOOR?!

...OKAY.

DING-DONG!

YOU WERE RIGHT, BUZZ! BEING A TOY IS THE BEST! ALL THE EXCITEMENT OF STAR COMMAND WITHOUT ANY *REAL* DANGER! I'M GONNA LOVE IT HERE!

JUST BE CAREFUL, BOOSTER! I SAW ANDY'S SISTER LOOKING YOU OVER EARLIER!

GLAD TO HEAR IT, BOOSTER.

I STILL REMEMBER THE TIME SHE CARRIED ME OFF TO HER ROOM...IT TOOK A WEEK FOR ANDY TO NOTICE I WAS MISSING!

AND EVEN LONGER TO DRAIN ALL THE DROOL OUT OF MY COIN SLOT!

IT WAS ONE TIME, HAMM. DON'T TAKE IT TO HEART. YOU AND I BOTH KNOW THAT ANDY LOVES Y--

ANDY, WHO'S AT THE DOOR?!

IT'S THE *POLICE!*

MA'AM, WE'D LIKE TO ASK YOU A FEW QUESTIONS ABOUT YOUR WHEREABOUTS LAST NIGHT?

....HIDE.

THE NEVER-ENDING TOY STORY...